THE "PERSONALISED" BOOK COMPANY

(THE BOOKS THAT MAKE "YOUR CHILD" THE STAR OF THE STORY)

FROM £ 5-95

CHILD'S NAME

AGE

ADDRESS

FRIENDS and/or RELATIVES

FAVOURITE PET or TOY

DEDICATION PAGE

EDUCATIONAL encourages/improves reading skills

HOURS OF FUN

ALL CHILDRENS BOOKS ARE IN FULL COLOUR WITH HARDBACKED WIPEABLE COVERS AND HANDBOUND TO LAST A LIFETIME

Contact/Office:

The Personalised Book Co.
23 Malvern Road, Wallasey
Merseyside L45 8NN
Telephone 051-639-9547

ORDER FORM FOR EVERY BOOK

IMPORTANT:PLEASE READ before completing your order.

We are restricted by the computer program as to how much information we can enter in any section.At the end of each line there is a number.**THIS IS THE MAXIMUM** amout of spaces we have for this entry.You must allow for commas or spaces to be inserted as well in the entry.If you exceed the number given we will not be able to print your book,as we will not know what to abbreviate or who to leave out.Also will you please **PRINT IN BLOCK CAPITALS THROUGHOUT THE FORM.**If you choose to write freehand and a mistake is made through your handwriting,we will not take resposibility for the error.

SECTION I COMPLETE FOR EVERY BOOK

MY CHOICE OF BOOK IS No.[ ]   IT IS FOR A   MALE [ ]

MY ALTERNATIVE CHOICE IS No.[ ]   FEMALE [ ]

FIRST NAME..(14)   SURNAME..............................(14)

POSTAL ADDRESS...(24)

THIS BOOK IS FROM...(22)

CHILD/PERSONS AGE WHEN BOOK IS TO BE GIVEN....................(10)whole years/months

DATE BOOK IS TO BE GIVEN..(14)

SECTION 2 FOR EVERY BOOK EXCEPT NEW BABY BOOK

FRIENDS and/or RELATIVES..(20)

You can have a favourite pet or toy included if you wish (this is optional),but they will run throughout the entire story:

NAME OF PET/TOY...(8) TYPE OF PET/TOY.................................(9)

FOR TEDDY BEARS PARTY ONLY: NAME OF TEDDY..(10)

FOR BIBLE STORY BOOK ONLY: NAME OF CHURCH...(16)

SOCCER HERO: Winners................................(20) Loosers............
MOVIE STAR: Film................................(20) Lead Role............(20)
SHOPPING SPREE: Dept.Store................................(20) Cafe............(20)
GOLF BOOK: Course................................(20) Competition............(18)
TENNIS BOOK: Tennis Star................................(20) Competition............(18)
FISHING BOOK: Type of Fish................(14) Length............(10) Weight............(10)
ROMANCE BOOK: Partners name................................(20)
AMERICAN FOOTBALL: Winners................................(18) Loosers............(18)

We do not need any information in this section for **OVER THE HILL BOOK**

SECTION 4 NEW BABY'S BOOK ONLY (WITH SECTION I ONLY)

DATE of BIRTH................(14) TIME of BIRTH............AM/PM WEIGHT............(20)

LENGTH............INS/CMS HOSPITAL................................(18) Tick if a single parent book [ ]

DELIVERED BY................................(12) DADS FIRST NAME............(12)

MUMS FIRST NAME................................

RETURN POSTAL ADDRESS................................

....

Your contact telephone number in case of query................................POST CODE............

POST CODE............

POST YOUR ORDER TO:
The Personalised Book Co.
23 Malvern Rd,Wallasey
Merseyside. L45 8NN
Telephone 051-639-9547

AMOUNT ENCLOSED

Book......£............
P.& Packing..0-80p
TOTAL............

PRICE LIST
YOGI/FLINTSTONES £6-95
NEW BABY BOOK £7-95
ALL OTHER TITLES £5-95

DO NOT SEND CASH Please make cheque/P.Order to **PERSONALISED BOOK CO.**

TITLES CURRENTLY AVAILABLE

[1] MY LITTLE MERMAID A girl becomes the beautiful mermaid, a boy the handsome prince. A shipwreck a life saving rescue plus of course the fairy tale ending

[2] TEDDY BEARS PARTY Your child has a magical trip with their teddy bear to the "Teddy's world jamboree", where teddies from all over the world meet for a big party.

[3] A SPACE ADVENTURE A daytrip to a space centre ends up with your child becoming a hero as they save the world from invasion by aliens from outer space.

[4] A DINOSAUR ADVENTURE Very much in the public eye of late, your child befriends "Nessie" the Dinosaur and they help Nessie to get rid of her nasty enemies.

[5] A BIRTHDAY WISH (Can only be given as a birthday present, owing to the story). Your child receives a mysterious parcel containing a magic lamp. A genie appears to make this the most exciting birthday ever.

[6] ROBIN HOOD ADVENTURE. Your child contiues the fight against the evil sheriff of Nottingham. A boy becomes Robin, a girl becomes Maid Marion as they break into the castle posing as musicians.

[7] MY GOOD EARTH. A day trip to the zoo to see the animals and your child becomes more aware of the importance of the environment, not only to animals but to the world in general.

[8] A CHRISTMAS STORY A dream come true for any child as they climb aboard Santa's sleigh on Christmas Eve. and help him to distribute presents all over the world following a trip to the grotto.

[9] A HANNUKAH STORY A touching story that will bring the true historical meaning of this festival to your child, relayed in a simple story form.

[10] NEW BABY BOOK A fabulous gift for any new parents (for less than the cost of a decent bunch of flowers). A full record of the birth of their child, with spaces for photographs, includes progress charts as well as spaces for recording presents and special milestones in baby's first two years. A gift to last a lifetime.

[11] MY BOOK OF BIBLE STORIES Includes verses from the old and new testaments.

[12] GET WELL SOON Lends a cheerful note to let that special person know it's not all that bad.

[13] FLINTSTONES ADVENTURE Your child joins Fred in his search for his loveable pet dinosaur "DINO" who seems to be lost or is he just playing with Fred.

[14] MY YOGI BEAR ADVENTURE Your child becomes the guest of honour at YOGI'S party in Jellystone Park

OLDER TITLES (OLDER CHILDREN OR HUMOROUS ADULTS)

[15] SOCCER HERO Line up with your favourite team against the team of your choice in The F.A. Cup Final. You never know, you just might score the winning goal in a tight match.

[16] MY SHOPPING SPREE Imagine being given £50,000 to spend in the department store of your choice. Fantasy it might be, but go on and enjoy it nevertheless, and then tell your friends over lunch.

[17] MY FISHING ADVENTURE Just imagine you are fishing for the biggest fish ever. You choose the Lake, the fish as well as size and weight! wonder if you really do catch "The really big one"

[18] MOVIE STAR ADVENTURE Ever dreamed of starring as the lead role in your favourite film. Now is your chance after being discovered when attending a celebrity party in Hollywood.

[19] THE GOLF STAR Winning a competition you get to play with the "Pro-stars" at the course of your choice in the competition of your choice. Will your nerve hold at the last green, can you sink that putt ??

[20] TENNIS STAR. Can you win the competition to play a set against your favourite star in the interval of a competition of your choice.? What's more if you can--how will you fare against them, is a win possible ?

[21] AMERICAN FOOTBALL STAR Line up with your favourite "grid-iron" team at The Superbowl against whoever you want. Surely you can't possibly score the winning touchdown, or can you ?
(DO NOT CONFUSE THIS BOOK WITH ENGLISH FOOTBALL---SEE SOCCER HERO)

[22] OVER THE HILL A light hearted look at the march of time for "the oldest swingers". Is a perfect gift for a birthday present if you have a sense of humour and perhaps want to give a "little dig"

[23 } MY ROMANTIC ADVENTURE Take a cruise to faraway places with that someone special . A story for the true romantics, choose your ideal partner for lots of fun and a very happy ending. Had a row ? Can't put your feelings into words ? Want to impress that some one special ?

We are continuously adding to our range, Please ring for a full update of all our titles currently available

ABOVE: *A presentation shawl, made in 1922 as a potential wedding present for Princess Mary, in the hands of the shawl dressers. Skilful finishing sets the pattern in place and brings out the full beauty of the lace. A detail of this shawl is shown on page 16.*

COVER: *A nineteenth-century Kilmarnock handknitted bonnet.*

SCOTTISH KNITTING

Helen Bennett

Shire Publications Ltd

CONTENTS

Set in 9 point Times roman and printed in Great Britain by C. I. Thomas & Sons (Haverfordwest) Ltd, Press Buildings, Merlins Bridge, Haverfordwest, Dyfed.

British Library Cataloguing in Publication Data available.

ACKNOWLEDGEMENTS

I am grateful to the knitters, owners of private collections and museum curators who have given their time and help, particularly: the Bishop of Leicester, Lady Veronica Gainford, Ms E. Kennedy, Miss I. D. J. Sandison, and the staffs of Gairloch Heritage Museum; Glasgow City Museums; the Dick Institute, Kilmarnock; the Royal Museums of Scotland; and Shetland Museum. Special thanks are due to Naomi Tarrant and Margaret Swain, and to my husband, Philip Bennett, for their advice and support.

Photographs on the following pages are reproduced by kind permission of: P. E. Bennett, page 23, Mr and Mrs Tam Dalyell of the Binns, page 26 (upper); the Dick Institute, Kilmarnock, page 5 (upper); Dumfries Museum, page 18; the Lord Forbes, page 24; Lady Veronica Gainford, pages 11 (right), 27; Glasgow City Museums, page 6 (lower); Miss M. J. Michie, page 17; National Galleries of Scotland, pages 9, 14 (right); Royal Museums of Scotland, cover and pages 1, 4, 6 (upper), 7, 8, 10, 13, 16, 19, 20, 21, 22, 25, 26 (lower); the Lady Saltoun, page 12; Miss I. D. J. Sandison, pages 14 (left), 15 (upper), 29; Scottish United Services Museum, Edinburgh, page 11 (left); Shetland County Museum, page 15 (lower); the Society of Free Fishermen of Newhaven, page 3; Mrs M. H. Swain, page 28; Lynda Usher, page 30. Other photographs are from the author's collection.

'Tartan' tammies being made on a warp knitting machine in Stewarton in 1976. The machine dates from the late nineteenth century, the period when mechanisation finally overtook hand methods in the Ayrshire bonnet industry.

A nineteenth-century fisherman from Newhaven on the river Forth. The young man's knitted bonnet and guernsey, one the work of a professional craftsman, the other made at home, are both personal ornament as well as effective protection against the elements.

INTRODUCTION

In the late fifteenth century knitted clothes, formerly great rarities, began to be made and worn in Scotland. Centuries passed before the new technique was commonplace in all parts of the country, yet gradually knitting became an integral part of Scottish life — as a means of clothing one's family against the northern climate, as a professional craft, as a method of paying the rent, and, eventually, as a pastime. A machine for knitting had been invented by an Englishman, the Reverend William Lee, in the time of Elizabeth I, and in Scotland a strong machine-based hosiery industry grew up from the eighteenth century. Even so, handknitting long retained its importance. It was handknitters, the principal heroes and heroines of this book, who developed the distinctive styles of knitting for which Scotland became famous.

BONNETS AND BONNETMAKERS

The earliest knitters in Scotland were not women knitting for their families but craftsmen working in Lowland towns. These professional knitters, called bonnetmakers, are first heard of in the fifteenth century. By 1496 the bonnetmakers of Dundee were sufficiently numerous to form a trade guild; within a hundred years similar incorporations had appeared in Edinburgh, Aberdeen, Perth, Stirling and Glasgow, and, a little later, in Kilmarnock and Stewarton in the south-west. As their name suggests, bonnetmakers manufactured the flat caps,

The technique of knitting allowed this man's woollen bonnet of about 1580 to be shaped and made in one piece without the cutting and sewing necessary with cloth. The ties-cum-earflaps were additions made by the wearer.

known locally as bonnets, which were fashionable menswear at the time. They also produced other knitted goods — stockings, gloves, sleeves and wylicoats, a kind of underclothing.

Bonnetmaking was a simple craft requiring inexpensive materials and little special equipment. The craftsmen worked solely with wool, generally the coarse fleeces unsuitable for weaving, which was prepared and spun into yarn by the women. The wool was knitted up on coarse needles and then the completed garments were pounded in water to shrink and thicken the fabric, a process known as waulking. Sometimes this was done by hand, although most bonnetmakers had access to a water-powered waulk mill. Finally, after drying to shape, the fabric was brushed with teazles to raise the nap, and trimmed with shears to give a felt-like finish.

In the form produced by the bonnetmakers, plain, heavy and inelastic, the new knitted clothing was not much admired by wealthier Scots, and generally the craftsmen were humble folk who earned at most a modest living. When John Nasmyth, a Glasgow bonnetmaker, died in March 1605, for example, the value of his movable belongings was estimated at only £77 Scots (£5-£6 sterling). Of this most was accounted for by eight dozen blue bonnets he had made, with 16 shillings for his tools — 'a dozen of bonnet brods', that is his knitting needles, and a pair of shears.

Against the odds, a few enterprising craftsmen made their fortunes. One such was Thomas Paterson, several times deacon of the Edinburgh bonnetmakers. Unlettered, unable even to sign his own name, he became an exceptionally wealthy man, leaving an estate, in 1616, of over £6000. He had been able to take advantage of the contemporary demand for boothose, the heavy overstockings used to protect expensive silk stockings from being damaged by their wearer's boots. The bonnetmakers' coarse stockings, otherwise known as Leith Wynd hose from the street in Edinburgh where many of the knitters lived, were ideal for the purpose. In partnership with three fellow craftsmen Thomas Paterson organised local production to such good effect that as many as fourteen thousand pairs were being shipped out every year, most bound for the Continent.

The products best suited to these work-

4

Massive needles were typical bonnetmaker's tools. The leather belt would have been worn at the waist to support the working needle and the often considerable weight of the bonnet.

ing methods were bonnets. These required a considerable weight of wool. From the records of the Dundee craft, for instance, we learn that in 1682 one Andrew Mill agreed to work for the master bonnetmaker David White for a year for a fee of £4 Scots, a pair of shoes, a pair of hose and a bonnet: his week's work was to make a dozen large bonnets, fifteen of the kind weighing 6 pounds (2.72 kg) a dozen, or twenty-two of the smallest, 4 pound (1.81 kg), size. Similar agreements show that large bonnets could weigh as much as 18 ounces (510 g). Knit in one piece and heavily waulked into a tight fabric, the bonnet was a solid and durable headcovering, an excellent protection against the Scottish weather: although out of fashion in Europe by 1600 it retained its popularity in Scot-

land. Worn by Highlander and Lowlander alike, it effectively became an item of national dress.

Originally bonnets were made in plain colours, blue being the favourite, and in one basic form. Set on a narrow headband, the crown might be little wider than the head, or sufficiently broad to shade the face of its wearer. It was not until the eighteenth century that new shapes appeared. In the army the bonnets of troops recruited in the Highlands at this time were gradually converted into an item of uniform. The headband deepened until the whole bonnet achieved a cylindrical or 'pork pie' shape, which was worn set up for full dress and unstiffened as a forage cap. This allowed room for distinguishing marks to be knitted in, such as rings to match regim-

French bonnetiers, professional knitters, in Diderot's 'Encyclopédie', 1763. The methods shown are similar to those used by Scottish bonnetmakers for finishing their knitted garments — fulling, drying on rigid shapes, and brushing and shearing the nap to produce a smooth outer surface.

5

ABOVE: *A man's bonnet of about 1715, made from blue woollen yarn with a decoration of red knots on the headband. Found on Lewis in the Western Isles, it would have been imported from one of the Lowland centres of bonnetmaking.*

BELOW: *Working men's woollen caps, such as this multicoloured example from Cambusnethan, were often known as Kilmarnock cauls or pirnies from the Ayrshire town where many were manufactured.*

From the mid eighteenth century bonnets became more varied in shape and decoration. This illustration, from James Logan's 'The Scottish Gael' (1831), shows a range of contemporary examples for both military and civilian use.

ental facings, chevrons, and the now famous diced band. The new styles were borrowed by civilians, who added further decoration; this was also the period at which the end of the yarn in the centre of the crown developed into the familiar red topknot or toorie.

In the late eighteenth century the industry was largely confined to Ayrshire. The demand for coarse hose, once exported as far afield as the West Indies, had long passed, and even the traditional bonnet market had wavered as the fashion-conscious young took to hats. While the craft elsewhere had declined to a small remnant, the knitters of Kilmarnock and Stewarton, in about 1720, had found a new product, the nightcap, which enabled them to survive the lean years. Roughly conical or bell-shaped, plain or striped, the nightcap was the everyday dress of working men and sailors.

A flourishing trade in military headgear also developed. Although the stiffened and befeathered dress bonnet remained peculiar to the Highland regiments, the forage cap was adopted by other Scottish units and, in the Victorian era, by English forces as well. In the late 1860s the annual value of bonnets and caps made in Kilmarnock, Stewarton and neighbouring Kilmaurs was said to surpass £145,000, occupying 3,300 women and girls as knitters and liners, and over three hundred men in finishing.

For centuries bonnetmaking had been almost entirely a hand craft. By the 1840s machine-spun yarn had been introduced, using Australian rather than local fleeces, but it was not until about 1870 that knitting machines operated by factory workers began to replace the old hand-knitters. Today the industry continues in Stewarton in its mechanised form. Tam o'Shanters, caps and balaclavas for sports and leisure wear are made, as well as bonnets for Scottish regiments, curlers, pipe bands the world over, and all who wear Highland dress.

7

Making stockings became an important source of extra income in many parts of Scotland, and the women knitted whenever their hands were free. Here, in 1902, two residents of the island of Foula, Shetland, knit while carrying peats for fuel.

Part of a sketch, 'Cottar's Saturday Night', by David Allan, about 1794. Knitting was a means by which even children, boys and girls alike, helped support the family. (National Galleries of Scotland, Edinburgh.)

STOCKINGS AND HOSE

By the seventeenth century the predominantly male, urban-based guilds of bonnetmakers had lost their monopoly: in town and country alike the technique of knitting was becoming more widely known and entering the female domain of domestic crafts. In consequence it was possible for new stocking industries to emerge, especially in eastern Scotland, based on the labour of women knitting at home.

About 1615 a traveller visiting Shetland, Richard Evans, noticed the abundance of sheep and the propensity of the women for knitting. Their stockings and mittens of home-grown wool were sold to visitors, particularly German traders, and the Dutch fishermen who came in their thousands every summer following the shoals of herring. Later, stockings were exported as makeweights with cargoes of cured fish to destinations as varied as

Hamburg, London and Oporto; in 1767 it was estimated that fifty thousand pairs, priced 6d each, were being sent out of the islands every year.

On the mainland the principal area of hosiery manufacture was Aberdeenshire. As early as 1636 a list of inhabitants of Old Aberdeen recorded several residents, women and children, whose occupation was given as 'shanker' (stocking knitter). Soon merchants were enlising women in rural areas too, supplying imported wool to be worked up to order and purchasing stockings made from local yarn. The products were then sent to England or the Continent.

For some, like the Aberdeen shankers, knitting was their main support. More often, particularly in the country, it was a means of supplementing family income: women, together with children, the elderly and the sick, knitted to pay the

9

land rent or to obtain goods they were unable to produce at home. To the admiration of visitors, who tended to contrast the apparent indolence of the men with the obvious industry of their womenfolk, knitting took up every spare moment. Worsted and 'wires' were taken out to be put to use in the fields at intervals of rest, and even when carrying loads or walking to market.

Most stockings seem to have come from the maker in the white, that is, undyed, but a variety of styles was knitted. Apart from the usual plain and ribbed there were also some more elaborate patterns: hosiery figured with squares was mentioned about 1745 as being made in Aberdeenshire in great quantity to please the Dutch market.

Quality varied dramatically, and there were constant efforts by those in authority to maintain at least a minimum standard. In 1720 Parliament found it necessary to stipulate that each pair of stockings made in Scotland for sale should be of one type of yarn and even workmanship throughout, free of such blatant faults as 'left loops, hanging hairs, and of burnt, cut or mended holes'. Yet some Scottish handknitters were capable of work of almost gossamer texture. The remarkable sum of 5 guineas was the value put on a pair of presentation stockings made in Aberdeen about this time. The stockings were reputedly so fine that the two together could be drawn through a thumb ring — a test of excellence for knitting which has lived on, at least in popular imagination.

The enthusiasm for handknitted hosiery was less apparent elsewhere in Scotland. In parts of the Highlands and Western Isles knitted garments continued to be rarities and many communities clung to the medieval-style stockings made from cloth. Even in the 1790s, the first Statistical Account records, the principal products of the parish of Comrie, Perthshire (now Tayside), were knee-length hose cut and sewn from tartan

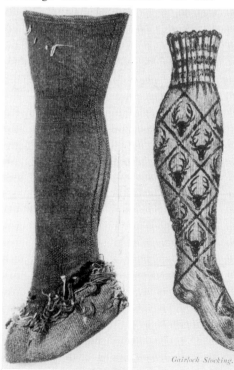

Gairloch Stocking.

FAR LEFT: *This stocking of natural brown wool is one of a group of knitted items from a late seventeenth-century grave discovered at Gunnister, Shetland. Although heavily worn and patched with rags, the excellence of the knitting is still apparent. (National Galleries of Scotland, Edinburgh.)*

LEFT: *The knitters of the west-coast parish of Gairloch became famous for highly-patterned short hose made for wearing with knickerbockers and kilts. This example appeared in 'Scottish Home Industries' published about 1895.*

LEFT: *The bonnet worn by this officer of the Black Watch, drawn by E. Dayes about 1790, would have been knitted in Ayrshire. Yet his red and white diced hose would still have been made in the medieval fashion, cut and sewn from cloth.*

RIGHT: *A sportsman, 1929. The fashion for wearing knickerbockers for outdoor pursuits, which began about 1860, brought skilfully knitted hose back to prominence in men's informal dress.*

fabric woven by the women.

Unlikely as knitting may seem as a vehicle for subduing an insurgent population, there had been continuing attempts to introduce the technique to the Highlands among measures to quash support for the exiled Stuarts in the wake of the 1715 and 1745 risings. The Gaelic speaking inhabitants, who preferred droving and hunting to more settled occupations, were regarded with suspicion by those living further south. There was a long-held view that by establishing schools to instruct the children in English and useful manufactures (such as stocking making) the Highlanders could be transformed

11

into obedient subjects of the Hanoverian monarchy.

Greater success in popularising knitting in the north and west was met with in the nineteenth century, particularly after the famine of 1846-8. To alleviate the distress of their tenants, benevolent landowners taught knitting to provide the women with an alternative source of income.

In the west-coast parish of Gairloch, Ross-shire (now Highland), a small industry initiated by Lady Mackenzie concentrated on men's fancy-patterned stockings. First worn with the kilt, they were soon to be fashionable with knickerbockers for outdoor pursuits. In this specialised area, where the handmade item was still often preferred to the factory-made product, the knitters were able to compete with the widely available machine-knitted hosiery, and Gairloch knitting flourished well into the 1900s.

The nineteenth century was also the period when knitting finally succeeded cutting and sewing in the making of the diced and tartan hose worn with Highland dress. Because the knitted examples usually follow the bias-cut cloth originals in that the pattern runs diagonally round the leg, several colours of yarn are required in one row. Most are therefore made according to a special technique which avoids the bulk caused by the usual method of stranding unused yarns behind the work. In this process, sometimes known as Argyll knitting, the garment is made flat on two needles rather than in the round and is worked with a separate ball of wool for each pattern area. Laborious to make, handknitted tartan hose were necessarily expensive and thus were usually replaced by plainer hose for everyday wear.

Tartan hose for wearing with a kilt (with a detail of the wrong side, right), knitted for the Master of Saltoun by his mother in the 1890s. Machine-made hosiery had long been available, but the making of stockings and socks for their families remained a matter of pride among Scottish women.

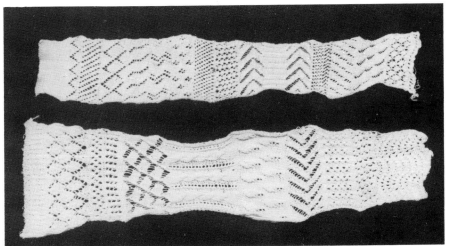

Early in the nineteenth century it was fashionable for knitted garments such as stockings to incorporate openwork designs of the type shown in these samplers. The delicate knitted lace of Shetland is a development of the same technique.

FINE SHAWLS AND LACE

In the early 1800s Shetland women, whose knitted goods had been sold abroad for at least two centuries, found that demand was failing. Their trade in stockings, caps and gloves, which had formerly brought £17,000 a year into the islands, had dwindled to less than a third. Knitting was done at home, supplementing a living gained from fishing and the croft: the problem, it seems, was that the traditional plain goods of the Shetlanders were no longer able to compete with frame-made hosiery now produced cheaply and in considerable quantity further south. In the face of the trend towards mass-production the Shetland industry might have fallen into permanent decline — but for the emergence of a new style, Shetland lace.

In keeping with the elaborate fashions of the time, lace of all kinds was highly popular throughout Europe in the nineteenth century. Knitwear too reflected this taste, in women's stockings and mittens, and in babywear patterned with lacy openwork stitches. At some time in the 1830s the idea was conceived of persuading Shetland women to turn their talents to knitting up the fine wool of the little native sheep into lace shawls: then the height of fashion for women, these could be expected to find a ready market outside the islands.

The identity of the originator of the plan is uncertain. What is known is that the persistent efforts of a few individuals, residents and visitors, were crucial in making known the new product and establishing a demand. On the northerly island of Unst, soon to be famous for lace, the Edmondston family took the lead in encouraging the knitters. Eliza Edmondston, wife of the local doctor, and herself an accomplished knitter, delighted in devising new patterns. Like her daughter, Jessie Saxby, Mrs Edmondston used her talent as a writer to publicise the work on the mainland. She also enlisted the help of friends there: residents in Edinburgh were asked to hold exhibitions of Shetland lace to stimulate orders, and others persuaded merchants to stock the goods.

Shetland lace seems to have been an almost immediate success. Early in the 1840s, aided by improved postal and steamer services, shawls and veils were already being exported in some quantity. Men's ties and other fancy goods, some in exotic yarns such as silk and mohair, soon

LEFT: *Mrs Jessie Saxby, photographed in 1891. A member of the Edmondston family of Unst, she was a talented writer and life-long champion of the Shetland knitters.*
RIGHT: *Miss Rigby (Lady Eastlake) pictured by pioneer photographer D. O. Hill in Edinburgh in the mid 1840s. Her fine knitted shawl may well have been made in Shetland, since at the time lace goods from the islands were being sent to the capital to be sold among well-to-do ladies. (National Galleries of Scotland, Edinburgh.)*

followed. Later the lace technique was applied to spencers (women's underbodices) and, from the 1920s, to jumpers and cardigans. Even curtains were knitted to order. Happily for the Shetlanders the notion was gaining ground that knitted garments were good for the health, so alongside the demand for the lace there was also a renewed interest in plainer work. By the end of the reign of Victoria a wide range of garments was being made in Shetland, notably underclothes, wraps for invalids and children's wear, the selling points of which were their exceptional softness and warmth.

Typically the web-like patterns were worked back and forth on two flexible metal needles on a ground of garter stitch. A single repeating motif might be used, particularly in heavier work, but many knitters took pleasure in inventing complex designs. The usual form for a fine shawl, for example, is an elaborately patterned middle, framed with a deep inner border which, in turn, is finished with a delicate vandyked edging, the whole so skilfully constructed as to appear seamless. Popular motifs include waves, fir trees, and the fiddle — a borrowing of the 'Paisley cone' so familiar from woven shawls. Since Shetlanders were not accustomed to using written instructions, designs were worked out by eye — a remarkable feat when one side of the border of a shawl might have four hundred stitches or more in a row.

When fresh from the needles, lace knitting appears a shapeless mass, and skilful finishing is required before its full beauty may be appreciated. First the work is washed and, where appropriate, bleached. Formerly knitting was hung in an enclosed space over smouldering sulphur to whiten in the fumes, although since the 1940s proprietary whiteners have gained favour. Originally, after rewashing, the shawls were staked out on grass to dry. From the end of the

ABOVE: *Knitted by Miss Jeanie Laurenson on Unst, this cotton blouse was made as a wedding present in 1921.*
BELOW: *When knitting for home use, Shetland women enjoyed devising special pieces, more varied than those made for sale. This tray cloth was made about 1920 by Miss Julia Sutherland, one of a family famous for their skill in fine knitting, from wool of her own spinning.*

ABOVE: *A scarf made at Balta Sound, Unst. Knitted in black and beige silk, rather than the usual wool, it is an example of the fancy goods produced for export to the mainland in the third quarter of the nineteenth century.*

LEFT: *This exceptionally fine shawl was one of two made as potential wedding gifts to Princess Mary from the women of Shetland in 1922. In the event this piece was not chosen, but was bought by a visitor and taken to Canada where, used for family christenings, it is treasured as an heirloom.*

16

nineteenth century, by which time shawl dressing had emerged as a specialist craft, it has been more usual to set the shawl on a frame. Each point of the shawl is threaded with a clean string and tied so that the whole work is stretched equally and achieves its proper form.

Fine knitting required the finest yarn, with great care taken at every stage of its making. Wool for the best-quality pieces was taken from the softest part of the fleece, on the throat of the sheep, by rooing (plucking) rather than clipping. Instead of being prepared by carding, the delicate fibres were straightened with a fine comb, or teased out with the fingers, before being spun up with a spindle or spinning wheel into the typical two-ply yarn. Smooth hands were essential for this task so particularly gifted spinners

might be relieved of rough work on the croft by other members of the family. In her *Sketches and Tales of the Shetland Islands* (1856) Mrs Edmondston noted that whereas a shawl generally required 4 to 5 ounces (110-140 g) of yarn, in the hands of the most expert spinners 6000 yards (5500 m) of thread, or enough for a good-sized shawl, could be spun from as little as 2 ounces (56 g) of wool.

Despite mechanisation, this art has never been lost. Although from about 1890 the wool grown in Shetland began to be sent to the mainland to be spun in the mills, a little continued to be handspun at home. Much of the demand for lace faded with the Victorian era. Yet a very small quantity of the finest yarn is still made by the old methods, and with it knitted lace of considerable excellence.

For this exquisite scarf Miss M. J. Michie of Edinburgh was awarded first prize for Shetland lace at the Royal Highland Show in 1979. Although now little made for commercial purposes, there is a continuing tradition of lace knitting in Scotland.

A sampler, the work of Miss Jessie Wilson of Sanquhar. The small patterns, typical of Sanquhar, bind the two yarns into a fine, close textured fabric.

LEFT: *The oldest known example of stranded knitting from Scotland; a brown wool purse patterned with pink and white, found at Gunnister, Shetland. A stocking from the same late seventeenth-century grave is shown on page 10.*
RIGHT: *Sanquhar gloves in dark blue and white two-ply wool, 1955. The Duke design, as this is known, is the most popular Sanquhar pattern with Scottish knitters.*

SANQUHAR AND FAIR ISLE

The simplest method of knitting a coloured pattern is to work together two threads of different colours, stranding the unused yarn behind the working yarn at each stitch. It is not surprising that this form of knitting is common in north-west Europe, for apart from its decorative possibilities there is the practical advantage that a fabric of double thickness is made. Worked in wool, the fabric is warm and durable yet flexible, an ideal protection against damp and cold. The discovery of a little patterned purse in a late seventeenth-century grave at Gunnister, Shetland, suggests that this useful technique was known in Scotland quite early, but another century may have passed before it became popular.

One version of this type of knitting is associated with the country town of Sanquhar in Dumfries and Galloway. In the 1790s the black-faced sheep outnumbered the human inhabitants of the parish by four to one, providing ample raw material for local woollen manufactures,

including stockings. According to Thomas Brown's *Union Gazeteer of Great Britain and Ireland* (1807), the stockings produced there were 'almost peculiar to the place...parti-coloured and of great variety of patterns'. Mittens and, rather later, gloves were made in the same manner. Thomas Brown does not mention whether the customer's name or initials were incorporated in the design, although this was a feature by the 1890s.

Sanquhar knitting is worked in two shades throughout. Black and white are the most common choice, although other combinations, such as yellow and brown or red and green, are sometimes found. Traditionally the knitter, using smooth yarns and very fine needles, around size 16 (1¼ mm diameter), works with one colour in each hand. The geometric patterns, which have a family resemblance to those of Cumbria and the Dales of England, are small and intricate: this ensures that the two yarns are woven into a close fabric, with no long strands

19

behind that might catch the toes and fingers of the wearer.

Today Sanquhar knitting is rarely made for sale. Nonetheless the style remains a favourite with keen knitters, its survival fostered by pattern leaflets published by the Scottish Women's Rural Institutes.

Perhaps the best known of all Scottish knitting originated from the opposite extremity of the country. Fair Isle, a small island set far out into the North Sea, halfway between Orkney and Shetland, shares the tradition, common to the northern isles, of knitting as a supplementary source of income to fishing and farming. Whereas the yarn used for Shetland knitting was mainly left in the whites, greys and browns natural to the native sheep, by the middle of the nineteenth century the inhabitants of Fair

Isle had become famous for their brightly dyed yarns and the intricacy of the designs they worked with them.

The earliest known examples of Fair Isle knitting are highly distinctive. Often they are figured with octagons, variously decorated, which are laid out in lines divided with bars and waves; vacant corners are filled with spot motifs. As in Sanquhar the stranded technique is used, but in Fair Isle the colour combination is changed every few rows, achieving a brilliant effect with just a few shades. Typically bands of blue and yellow alternate with others of red and white. Yellow was dyed with onion skins or island plants, while red and blue were generally obtained with imported substances, madder and indigo, bought through the island shop. Indigo in particular was expensive, and brown wool was sometimes substi-

LEFT: *One of the earliest surviving pieces of Fair Isle knitting, a sampler in red, white, blue and yellow wool, presented to the Industrial Museum of Scotland (later the Royal Scottish Museum) in 1858.*

RIGHT: *This child's purse in brightly coloured silks is a drawing room version of Fair Isle knitting, thought to have been made in Orkney about 1850.*

A Mr Jamieson of Unst, Shetland, photographed early in the twentieth century wearing a Fair Isle jersey and cap.

tuted for blue for economy.

Although examples had been shown at the Great Exhibition of 1851 and on other occasions on the mainland, until well into the twentieth century Fair Isle knitting seems to have had little more than local currency. The main items produced were jerseys for men, scarves, gloves and long pointed caps patterned round the brim. The jerseys and caps were favoured by seamen and were sometimes traded with the crews of passing vessels for salt, meat and biscuits. More often, the garments were sold through shops in Kirkwall and Lerwick, where they were bought by tourists as curiosities.

About 1920 Fair Isle was 'discovered' by the outside world. Knitwear had become a fashionable commodity, and

ABOVE: *A Fair Isle scarf in red, white, yellow and brown wool, bought by a tourist in Kirkwall, Orkney, about 1910.*

BELOW: *A double page from one of the pattern books published by R. Williamson of Commercial Street, Lerwick, 1927-33. Many of the books are still in use among Shetland knitters.*

The reverse of a slipover in 'natural' shades by 'Shetlands from Shetland'. It was made for the London market in 1975 at a time when, once again, Fair Isle had achieved the status of high fashion.

the island's coloured patterns were suddenly in vogue. Their popularity was confirmed when the Prince of Wales played golf dressed in Fair Isle jersey and hose. To meet the unprecedented demand, knitters all over Shetland took up the work.

From this time both the colours and the patterns became more varied. Pattern books had rarely been used in the islands, but it occurred to a Lerwick man, Bobby Williamson, that since many were new to this style of knitting there was scope for a book of motifs suitable for inclusion in Fair Isle garments. Between 1927 and 1933, with the aid of a local girl, Mary Johnstone, and her brother, designs were stencilled in red and green dots into graph exercise books, which were then sold through Mr Williamson's shop in Commercial Street. Apart from motifs already current in Shetland knitting, many from other sources were included which have now become incorporated in the Fair Isle tradition.

Since the 1920s interest in the Fair Isle style, although fluctuating, has never entirely abated. Numerous commercial patterns have been printed, and factory-made adaptations have been produced in Britain and elsewhere. Thus, although knitwear of this kind has continued to be made in the northern isles, Fair Isle has become part of the repertoire of knitters throughout the world.

When Lady Caroline Hunter sat for her portrait about 1760, she chose to be shown engaged in the, by then, common domestic activity of knitting. She is making a stocking or perhaps a long nightcap.

A hen's feather knitting sheath similar to that in the portrait of Lady Caroline Hunter (behind her right arm). Tucked into the apron strings as a support for the working needle, it helped the knitter to work faster and keep the stitches even. This example was made in Orkney about 1950.

KNITTING FOR HOME AND FAMILY

First introduced to Scotland as a professional craft about the time of James IV, by the reign of George III, some two and a half centuries later, knitting had become an everyday domestic activity. Just as girls had long been trained in spinning and sewing to prepare them for clothing their own families, so now the competent housewife was also expected to be a dextrous knitter. Nor did well-born ladies disdain the accomplishment. Lady Mary Drummond, daughter of the Duke of Perth, is reputed to have been particularly skilled with her needles: about 1733, according to Kennedy's *Annals of Aberdeen,* she made three pairs of gloves so fine that they could have been sold for the luxury price of three guineas a pair.

For family use stockings were most in demand, together with nightcaps, gloves and other small items such as garters. Although jackets and waistcoats were sometimes made, to be worn under other clothes for warmth, knitted main garments were not common. For yarn the knitter had wool and linen, perhaps from sheep or flax of her own raising. Cotton, which was confined mainly to well-to-do households, was bought ready spun. Silk too was available but was expensive and little used for this purpose since the Scottish housewife was knitting more

with a view to economy and hard wear than to decorative effect.

For centuries the methods of working must have been passed on by one person teaching another, and new patterns learnt by eye from knitted-up samples, for instructions were rarely written down. Indeed it was not until the Victorian era that printed pattern books for knitting came into wide circulation. Among the pioneers was Mrs Jane Gaugain, whose *Lady's Assistant for Executing Useful and Fancy Designs in Knitting, Netting and Crochet* was first published in 1840. Eventually extended to three volumes, *The Lady's Assistant* became a best-seller and was still being re-issued twenty-five years later, long after the author's death.

Mrs Gaugain was the proprietor of 'the Foreign and British Depot of Berlin Patterns and Materials for Lady's Fancy Works', in George Street, a fashionable location in Edinburgh's New Town. In business with her husband, probably since the mid 1820s, Mrs Gaugain seems to have enjoyed the patronage of a number of society ladies and to have been held in some respect; in 1842 she was recommended as a suitable arbiter in a dispute between the Duchess of Buccleuch and a local firm of embroiderers. Apart from supplying needlework mate-

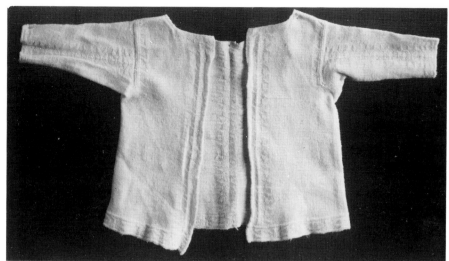

ABOVE: *A cotton jacket from a mid eighteenth century layette at the House of the Binns. An enthusiasm for knitted garments, particularly of wool, as promoters of health, did not emerge until the nineteenth century. Before then comparatively little use was made of knitting for babywear.*

BELOW: *This pair of slipper socks, made in brightly coloured commercial wools, is a rare example of the fancy work popular as a drawing room pastime in the 1840s. The design incorporates small motifs similar to those described by Mrs Gaugain in 'The Lady's Assistant'.*

26

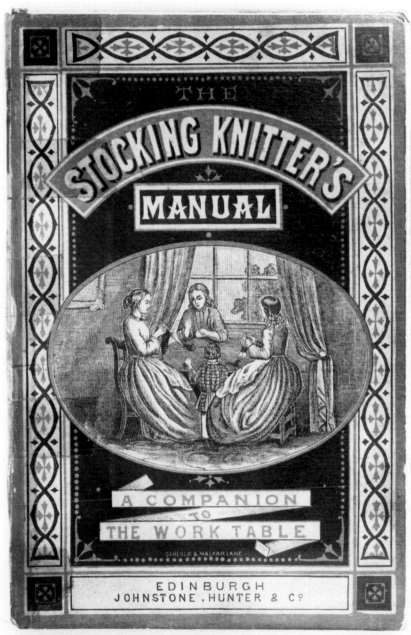

Patterns were passed on by example from knitter to knitter/ until the 1840s, when printed instructions became more common. This pattern book, published in Edinburgh in 1867, was intended for teachers as well as domestic knitters.

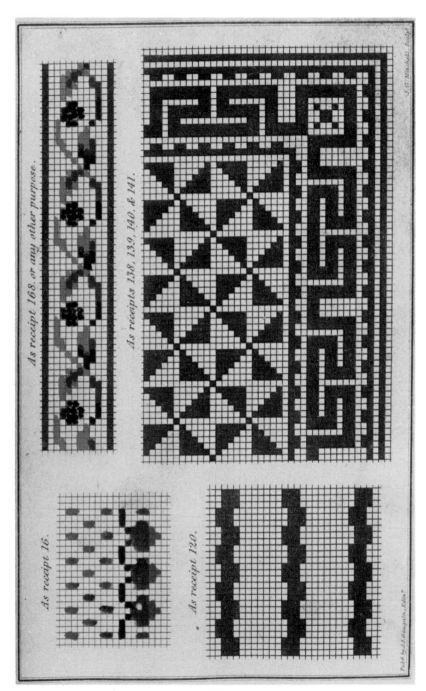

As receipt 168. or any other purpose.

As receipts 138, 139, 140. & 141.

As receipt 16.

As receipt 120.

J.G. Mitchell. Sculp.

Pub.d by J.Johnstone, Edin.r

28

rials, such as patterns for the currently popular Berlin work (wool embroidery on canvas), Mrs Gaugain also offered lessons — and her experience as a teacher is surely reflected in her writing. At a time when knitting instructions were vague and far from standardised, her books were full of practical comments. She was careful to specify the exact materials to be used and was unusual in recommending her readers to obtain a wire-drawer's gauge, the original of the modern knitting gauge, to ensure that their needles were of the correct diameter. Sizing of garments, though, was at best approximate, and the idea of knitting a tension square to ensure a correct fit took another fifty years and more to emerge.

The mass of instruction books published in the 1840s and 1850s coincided with a craze for knitting as an elegant pastime. Because of industrialisation, yarns in a wonderful variety of shades and fibres were readily available. With these materials for inspiration, and time on their hands, leisured Victorian ladies had opportunities to experiment unthought of by their predecessors. To the twentieth-century eye some of the pro-

OPPOSITE: *A page of designs from volume II of 'The Lady's Assistant' (1842). The figures could be used for various handicrafts: that on the upper right was recommended for items as varied as a baby's knit blanket, a crochet bag, and a tablecover worked in cross-stitch on canvas.*

BELOW: *Eliza Macbriar Edmondston, about 1865. Well known as a friend of the Shetland lace knitters, she was herself an accomplished knitter. The two woollen rugs were made in a technique of her own devising, a version of what was then termed tapestry knitting, which allows the two sides of the work to appear almost identical.*

ducts of their ingenuity appear of doubtful elegance and still less utility. Yet this must be recognised as the period when knitting as a domestic craft reached full maturity. Knitting with two or more colours, lace and patterned work in general were developed and perfected, providing a rich legacy of stitches and techniques for the modern knitter. Among the entries for the Great Exhibition of 1851 is listed 'a landscape knitted in Berlin worsteds', the invention of an Aberdeen lady. So it seems that even the 1970s passion for landscape knitting was anticipated.

The pattern books show that the use of knitting was being extended. To furnish the home, there were designs for coverlets and counterpanes, cushions and curtains, as well as a miscellany of doyleys and trimmings. For clothing, in addition to the items traditional to the knitter, Mrs Gaugain and her contemporaries provided instructions for collars and cuffs, underwear, shawls and accessories such as muffs. There are also patterns for jackets and waistcoats which were intended to be worn visibly. These last, however, are occasional and, one suspects, little used. In some seafaring communities the fisherman's knitted frock, once an item of underclothing, had emerged as a working garment. This specialist use apart, jerseys were considered most suitable for the sports field. It was not until the 1920s, when knitwear became high fashion, that knitted main garments achieved a prominent place in the output of the domestic knitter.

'Trellis' cardigan handknitted in silk. One of the 1985 range of knitwear designs by Lynda Usher of Invermoriston, Inverness-shire.

POSTSCRIPT

Despite the availability of a broad range of mass-produced clothing and the prominence of factory-knitted fabrics and garments, knitting remains a popular activity in Scotland. Undoubtedly the most influential contribution of the twentieth century has been the development of the domestic knitting machine. A number of small cylinder models, capable of making socks and stockings, were available by the late Victorian period and were used in some Scottish households. It was not, however, until the end of the 1930s that the first of the modern knitting machines appeared, and longer still before they were widely used. Handknitting is rarely commercially viable today — except perhaps for the luxury market. But the advent of versatile portable machines, which allow the speedy production of small runs or individually designed garments, has stimulated rather than destroyed knitting as a craft industry. In the home both hand and machine methods are being used to re-interpret traditional styles and explore new possibilities.

'Trees and Sheep' landscape waistcoat in green, grey and brown wool made by Margaret Hyne of Glenbuchat, Aberdeenshire, in 1980; an example of knitwear made on a domestic machine for the craft market.

FURTHER READING

Barnes, Ishbel. 'The Aberdeen Stocking Trade'. *Textile History,* volume 8 (1977), 77-98.

Bennett, Helen. 'The Scots Bonnet' in *From the Stone Age to the 'Forty-Five,* edited by O'Connor and Clarke. John Donald, 1983.

Gainford, Veronica. *Designs for Knitting Kilt Hose and Knickerbocker Stockings.* Published by the author and the Scottish Development Agency, not dated.

Gulvin, Clifford. *The Scottish Hosiery and Knitwear Industry.* John Donald, 1984. An account of the machine-based part of the industry only.

Henshall, A., and Maxwell, S. 'Clothing and Other Articles from a Late Seventeenth-Century Grave at Gunnister, Shetland'. *Proceedings of the Society of Antiquaries of Scotland,* volume 86 (1951-2), 30-42.

McGregor, Sheila. *The Complete Book of Traditional Fair Isle Knitting.* Batsford, 1981.

Smith, M., and Twatt, M. *A Shetland Pattern Book.* The Shetland Times Ltd, Lerwick, 1979.

PLACES TO VISIT

Modern museum practice avoids the long-term exhibition of textiles, so knitted items are rarely to be found on permanent display. It is therefore essential to write in advance for permission to see knitting.

The most extensive collection of Scottish knitting is to be found in the former National Museum of Antiquities of Scotland which, at the time of writing, is in the process of amalgamation with the Royal Scottish Museum, Edinburgh. Enquiries should be directed to:

Royal Museums of Scotland, Chambers Street, Edinburgh EH1 1JF. Telephone: 031-225 7534.

Other collections are held at:

Dumfries Museum, The Observatory, Church Street, Dumfries DG2 7SW. Telephone: Dumfries (0387) 53374.

Glasgow Art Gallery and Museum, Kelvingrove, Glasgow G3 8AG. Telephone: 041-357 3929.

Museum of Costume, Camphill House, Queen's Park, Pollokshaws Road, Glasgow G41 2EW. Telephone: 041-632 1350.

Sanquhar Museum, The Tolbooth, Sanquhar, Dumfrieshire. Telephone: Sanquhar (065 92) 303 or contact Dumfries Museum, as above.

Shetland Museum, Lower Hillhead, Lerwick, Shetland ZE1 0EL. Telephone: Lerwick (0595) 5057.